What Is a Garden?

What Is a Garden?

POEMS AND ESSAYS BY W. S. Merwin   PHOTOGRAPHS BY

Larry Cameron

THE UNIVERSITY OF SOUTH CAROLINA PRESS

Published by the University of South Carolina Press
Columbia, South Carolina 29208

www.sc.edu/uscpress

Manufactured in China

25 24 23 22 21 20 19 18 17 16
10 9 8 7 6 5 4 3 2 1

Library of Congress Cataloging-in-Publication Data
Merwin, W. S. (William Stanley), 1927–
 [Works. Selections]
 What is a garden? / W. S. Merwin ; photographs by Larry Cameron.
    pages ; cm
 "Poems and essays."
  ISBN 978-1-61117-567-7 (hardcover)
 I. Title.
 PS3563.E75A6 2015
 818'.54—dc23
 2015022502

Palm identifications that are not by W. S. Merwin are courtesy of Dr. John Dransfield, honorary research fellow, Herbarium Royal Botanic Gardens, Kew, United Kingdom; and Dr. David Lorence, codirector of science and conservation, National Tropical Botanical Garden, Kalaheo, Hawaii.

Archival photographs courtesy of the Alexander & Baldwin Sugar Museum, Puunene, Hawaii, and the Maui Historical Society, Bailey House Museum, Wailuku, Hawaii.

CONTENTS

vii Introduction: This Garden

1 What Is a Garden?

11 Coming to Palms

47 Rain Light

49 Rain at Night

51 The Shape of Water

79 Native Trees

81 To Lili's Walk

83 The House and Garden:
     The Emergence of a Dream

113 The Laughing Thrush

115 To Paula in Late Spring

117 Place

119 Photographer's Notes

123 Key to the Palms

v

INTRODUCTION

This Garden

The first time I saw the land here it did not look like a garden. It was on an afternoon late in August, thirty-some years ago. I know now that it was late in the month because pairs of plover sailed over me, repeating their two call notes just above me. Calls of rejoicing, at that moment, celebrating their return home from the summer months of nesting and raising their fledgling chicks on their nests out on the tundra. The last part of their return had been more than a seven hundred-mile flight from the coast of Alaska to the sea cliffs at the end of the dirt track a quarter of a mile past the turn-off onto this land. The plovers flying just above me, and their celebration of being home, were my welcome to the place. The place itself did not look particularly welcoming. That part of the north coast of Maui, which in Hawaiian is called the Hamakua Loa, the "long corner," is a series of small valleys running like veins down the skirt of the great mountain, Haleakala, which in English means "House of the Sun." When I stood there the ridges were bare except for the dry grasses of the end of summer. Almost no trees except for the wild common mango trees along the stream bed. The stream bed lay just below me, Peahi Kahawai (the beautiful word *kahawai*, for stream bed, was given by the Caucasian settlers the ugly word "gulch," a bit of jargon from the western mining camps).

I had been told about this bit of land by a woman friend who knew I was looking for somewhere to live on this part of Maui. She had heard about it herself from a friend who had told her that the cabin on the land, which I could see a hundred yards or so ahead of me beside the entrance track, had been the hiding place of three of the young Hawaiian and Caucasian activists who had occupied the island of Kaho'olawe, the small island off the coast of Maui. Kaho'olawe was sacred to the Hawaiians. The U.S. Navy had confiscated it after Pearl Harbor, and had used it for maneuvers, practice landings, and bombing practice all through the war. The Hawaiians wanted the Navy's use of the island to be stopped and they wanted the island back. The group of young men had "invaded" the island and informed the Navy that they were there and would not leave. The Navy tried to dislodge them but the young rebels stayed on for some days, until the Navy took dogs over to find and arrest them, and the young men slipped away at night and returned to Maui on their surfboards. Three of them had made their way to this cabin. I looked at it, and then walked to the beginning of the slope down into the small valley. Stepping into the shadow of the mango limbs, I was in another world. It was cool and had a kind of secrecy to it, a silence that, as I saw when I walked a little farther down the slope, arose from the fact that there was no water flowing in the rock-lined *kahawai*. The stream, as I would learn, had been effectively cut off by the sugar planters a hundred years earlier. They had been taking the water along that coast for decades by then, to divert it to their vast sugar plantations on the isthmus of the island, and to simultaneously drive the Hawaiians out of the valleys where they kept their taro fields and family patches of banana and papaya trees. As I stood under the mangos, that afternoon, a thrush began singing in the branches just above me. His voice, and the cries of the plovers on the dirt road earlier, spoke to me of the life of the place, just

there and just then, and I felt a wish to have more to do with it. That moment went with me as I went back up the hill.

I learned the history of that piece of land by asking a few questions of the people who lived out along the coast. It was ruined soil, as I could see, up near the entrance. In the country records it was - and still is, described as a wasteland, with a hand-scrawled note below it saying "nothing will grow here." Once, until the middle of the nineteenth century, this land had been a forest. The mixed indigenous Hawaiian trees, principally the Hawaiian koa—*Acaci koa*—had been clear-cut to build houses for the missionary settlement at Lahaina on the south coast, and then for firewood for the settlers and for the whaling vessels that began to anchor there to take on supplies for their voyages.

When the forest was gone from this bit of the north coast, cattle were turned out to graze, but without great success. With the tree canopy gone, the tropical sun parched the remaining humus and it washed and blew away. There were attempts to extend the sugar growing out along the coast—there was even a single railroad line for transporting the cane. But the yield was too small to pay for the venture and it was abandoned and turned over again, for a while, to scrawny cattle. A final venture between World War I and Pearl Harbor arose when several enterprising but naïve hopefuls had the idea of buying the whole valley, dirt-cheap as the phrase has it, to grow the latest profitable introduction: pineapple. They bought the valley, built a fan of access tracks on both slopes, and then proceeded to plow both slopes vertically so that any remaining topsoil washed away in the first heavy rains, and once again the land was simply abandoned. When I first saw the valley there were very few people living here, and what they lived in was tucked away in the folds of the slopes; a few people lived in packing cases, one or two others in structures made of salvaged pieces of rusted metal roofing. The cabin here had been built by its former owner, an Australian construction engineer, and it actually had a building permit, which may have been unique in the area. I was not discouraged by the fact that the soil was ruined. I had long wanted to restore a piece of ruined land.

In my twenties, when I was spending winters in London, I had been part of the early anti-nuclear movement. I had come to see the evils of the use of nuclear energy, and chemical agriculture, which prepared the soil by poisoning it, and used poisons throughout the growth of the crop. I read about the English Soil Movement and ate the products that were available in London.

One day in the Sunday papers there was an advertisement offering for sale a recently converted sheep barn near the valley of the Dordogne in southwest France. I was living in the house of an English woman, who had visited that part of France and fallen in love with it. I had an old car. We decided to drive down and see the fixed-up sheep barn and the region. The sheep barn had nothing to recommend it. But the man who had placed the ad in the English paper did interest me. He must have been around seventy: gray-white beard on his long, lean face. He looked to me like pictures I had seen of the aging D. H. Lawrence. His name was Philip Oyler. He had been an agronomist and was one of the founding members of the Soil Movement. In retirement he had driven south in France until he found the small farming village where he had settled and had become part of the village and of a way of life that seemed to have become extinct in much of the rest of the world. He wrote about it in a book called *The Generous Earth*. I learned from what I saw of his way of life, his garden, his story.

My companion and I were staying in a small hotel across the river. Every morning the hotel packed a picnic lunch and we set off to explore the region. I was drawn especially to the limestone upland. One day we drove along a dirt road at the top of the ridge and passed a small forest of ancient oak trees, emerging to a vast view of the entire valley of Dordogne, four hundred feet below us. Ahead of us was the beginning of a small farming hamlet. My companion and I set out to explore different directions, as we did usually. She walked farther upland; I went toward the hamlet past two ancient stone barns, apparently empty. And just beyond them I saw a small, apparently ancient stone farmhouse that appeared to have been unlived-in for a very long time. Brambles and ivy overran the roof and there were tiles missing. I walked down the dirt road to the house perched on the ridge, its other side overlooking the great valley. There was a hole in the wall where a stone or brick had fallen out, and I made my way through the brambles and looked in onto a floor littered with broken plaster rubble. There were swallows' nests in the rough oak beams. On the far side of the room was an arch with an alcove beyond it and a small window that must have looked out over the valley and the river.

A voice behind me said, in the local accent, "Are you looking for something?"

I turned and saw an old man, evidently from the village, coming from work—he was holding a pitchfork—on his way home for the midday *soupe*. I said "I was just looking at this house."

He said, "It's old."

I said, "It looks as though no one has lived in it for a long time."

He said, "Long time."

It turned out to belong to a Mme. Bergougnoux. I went to see her, and asked if she would sell it. Her asking price, which was the same as she had made to an English woman before the war, was a figure that amounted, in dollars, to $1,200. That was exactly the value of the tiny legacy that had been left to me by my mother's older second cousin, a retired schoolteacher. I felt that my aunt was offering me the French house, and with the wisdom of another world, knew how important it would be to me: my own house, deep in the countryside in southwest France. I shook Mme. Bergougnoux's hand, all an irrevocable agreement needed in that society, and bought the property—house, barns, land, garden. I drove north for the city winter without pausing to dwell upon the fact that the transaction, the price, and the attitudes of Mme. Bergougnoux and her husband represented the end of an age. That winter I worked hard for the BBC Third Programme, earning money to fix the roof and floors and build a water containment cistern with a terrace on top of it on the north side of the house.

For years I spent the months of spring to autumn working in the garden, growing all the vegetables that we ate there. I spent those winters in London and then in New York earning money with odd bits of writing. That French village garden and what I had learned from it were what I brought with me to the land here in Hawaii.

As I said earlier, I had two things I hoped to do with the land here: restore the ruined soil, and restore a section of indigenous Hawaiian forest that had grown here before the Caucasians arrived and deforested the Hamakua Loa, the "long corner" of the north coast. For the first of them, on the day I signed the escrow papers, I came back over here (before long I would say "I came home here") and planted the first trees up along the dirt road. They were *Casuarinas*—sometimes called "ironwoods" or "weeping pines." A friend had potted up several of two species, *equisetifolia* and *cunninghamia,* in tall coffee cans, and he was moving away. The choice of species was important. The State Agricultural Department for several years had been giving away, in a reforestation project, seedlings of *Cunninghamia glauca* whose surface roots send up parades of suckers, and the species gave all *Casuarina glauca* a bad name for a while. The *equisetifolia* and the *cunninghamia* have no such disadvantages, and the genus is known to be one of the only kinds of trees besides the legumes that draws nitrogen and oxygen out of the air to its own roots and builds new humus at its base. From the way the *Casuarinas* grew here—ten feet a year, to their full, towering ninety-five—I thought they must be doing that (I heard rumors of people growing strawberries around the bases of the trees, watering them by hand). I learned the full truth nearly thirty years later, when they were attacked by termites. Great branches as thick as thighs, twenty-five feet long and weighing eighty pounds, came crashing down on smaller palms growing near them. If they had landed on someone the impact could have been fatal. The great trees had to be taken down. I dug my long planting spade into the ground a foot or so from one of the stumps and it sank into black humus more than two feet deep. New soil, full of life. And the new soil with its soil organisms spread and nurtured palm seedlings all along the slope. The restoration of the soil, begun by the *Casuarinas*, had spread by itself and continues to do so.

But I had come to realize that I could not restore the destroyed native forest. Ray Baker, of the Lyon Arboretum, told me that no one could do that because exotic invasive species had been introduced, and introduced insects, fungi, and pests of all kinds that had not been in the old habitats now lived there. But I have come to recognize that no human being can plant any forest. A forest is not made by a human being planting a few trees. It evolves as a complex society of soil organisms, and other plants besides trees. (The great American prophet Henry David Thoreau was pondering some of these matters on his death bed.) Only a forest can restore a forest—a section of forest that had once grown beside it. Our human destructions are often irreparable, like the extinction of species.

The native forest I had hoped to re-create I learned was impossible. The one native plant that seemed able to survive and grow here was the Hawaiian palm, the genus *Pritchardia*. I began planting *Pritchardia*, then realized that palms were endangered everywhere in the world, and I began to plant palms from elsewhere, growing them often from seed or from seedlings bought from growers. I tried to plant them in what I hoped would be forest conditions, close together to restore the forest canopy. Over these thirty years, they have come to be a forest, and it surprises me every day.

What Is a Garden?

All day working happily down near the stream bed
  the light passing into the remote opalescence
it returns to as the year wakes toward winter
  a season of rain in a year already rich
in rain with masked light emerging on all sides
  In the new leaves of the palms quietly waving
time of mud and slipping of overhearing
  the water under the sloped ground going on whispering
as it travels time of rain thundering at night
  and of rocks rolling and echoing in the torrent
and of looking up after noon through the high branches
  to see fine rain drifting across the sunlight
over the valley that was abused and at last left
  to fill with thickets of rampant aliens
bringing habits but no stories under the mango trees
  already vast as clouds there I keep discovering
beneath the tangle the ancient shaping of water
  to which the light of an hour comes back as to a secret
and there I planted young palms in places I had not pondered
  until then I imagined their roots setting out in the dark
knowing without knowledge I kept trying to see them standing
  in that bend of the valley in the light that would come

4

6

Coming to Palms

Some time after midnight the wind drops and the silence wakes me.

The bare wooden floor shines like a sky. The moon is nearly full. After the rain the banana leaves outside the long windows are leaning mirrors reflecting only light. I get up and walk out into the trees.

On the slope the monkeypods that I planted as seedlings no taller than chives tower above the house. Their paired leaflets the size of thumbprints close like books with the approach of night, so that stars and the barely moving clouds appear through the veinwork of branches. The moonlight reaches through to whiten night-blooming jasmine, plumerias, and understory palms.

The lane of bright grass leading seaward disappears under glittering arches formed by the long fronds of young coconut palms. The oldest of them, planted in the same winter as the monkeypods, are just beginning to develop trunks, but the leaves still look as though they rose directly from the ground into massive fountains. A few leaflets catch a breeze and rattle. Those coconuts were the first palms I set in the ground almost twelve years ago. I was so ignorant then that I scarcely knew other kinds of palms existed, or that there were different strains and varieties of coconuts as there are of roses and dogs, each with its place of origin, its virtues and adherents. Or that there is a whole lore of coconuts that recounts the birth of some of them, in Tahiti, from the heads of children who died of hunger, and tells of others that grew from the heads of fishermen who had dangled their hair in the sea as bait, and of some that sprang from the heads of gods. Heads, though, again and again. In Hawaii the lore includes legends associating the tree's arrival with the gods Kane and Kanaloa and its body with the god Ku. I had no idea what I was planting.

It is just as well I began with coconut palms, which in the tropics are said to be able to grow virtually anywhere (or were able to until the virus disease known as Lethal Yellows began wiping them out around the Caribbean in the seventies). Coconuts do not even have to be planted if they land somewhere shady and damp when they fall. In a matter of weeks or months, depending on the season and the maturity of the nut, the first wiry orange-yellow roots emerge and reach downward to the earth, and the pointed bundle that will unfold into two leaves like the ears of a green hare sprout at the rounded end and curve upward. In a remarkably short time the roots anchor themselves so tightly in the soil that they seem inseparable from it, and begin to feed a growing tree. Even so, a coconut's future is more secure if it is planted in good soil and not completely covered. Some say that the partly exposed nut should lie to the south of the leaves, to catch the sun, but I have not noticed that anyone is very particular about that. The ancient Hawaiians planted an octopus under the nut. The octopus is one of the manifestations of the primeval creation god Kanaloa, who in Hawaii is the deity of the West, of the sea, and of death. It is said that the octopus under the coconut represented a hope that the tree would cling like tentacles. All I learned at the time when I planted those first coconuts was that it was important not to let the grass smother the seed, and to keep cattle from eating the leaves. From the moment

they began to grow, they would be native to the spot, in one sense at least, as I could never be.

I was not born in a place that suggested the likelihood of wandering in the moonlight, some time later, looking at palms. I suppose my ignorance when I planted these coconuts was something that would be called normal at present, even natural, given my own origins, which surrounded me with the insistence that they were ordinary to the point of being absolute, and therefore unnotable. It was taken for granted that everyone lived in rooms, clothes, habits like those I could see, and was urban, middle-class, northeastern American. The world was the New Jersey hinterland and the minor industrial towns of Pennsylvania, the crimped, seamless propriety of a poorly paid minister's family in the years of the Depression. At the age of two I stared from my brown wicker baby carriage at the closed brass doors of a bank without knowing what they were, but I can still feel the sense of shock and helpless loss hovering before them, and remember my mother silently crying.

There was never much money, and it is remarkable that we managed to go anywhere at all. We did have a car though, even then, and we drove across Pennsylvania from time to time to visit my father's family north of Pittsburgh. I saw hills covered with trees and wanted to go to them as we passed. And when I was three we went for a winter or more to St. Petersburg, Florida, a move that we were all convinced was essential to my father's health. He had been so sick that the suit had been bought in which he was to be buried, and while we were in Florida he was enveloped in flannels and tones of invalidism and was congratulated when he walked out of doors.

Coconuts

Indians in Winter Camp

We lived in a bungalow on a side street and went out very little. I knew no other children my own age, and there was nowhere to play except in the narrow yard. We took walks to the end of the block where there was a grapefruit orchard to look at. I mention that time because it was my first glimpse of anywhere remotely tropical and would be the only sight of the tropics I would have for a long time, and I cannot say that it made any distinct impression on me. It was the way the world was, for a while. A train made of newspapers laid out on the living room floor in late afternoon. A sunny porch and breakfast with honey out of a blue can with a bee on it. A chimpanzee (I suppose) chained to a platform in a vacant lot. We saw palms, I know, because they were growing dim against the oyster shell twilight in the darkening photographs my mother took at the time. They must have seemed to be details of the general strangeness, like unfamiliar wallpaper. But then there were the woods that I watched with hypnotized fascination from the train, on the way north, as I was coming down with a fever that would become pneumonia. I return to the image of them as I try to find some source for the love of trees and woods, the recurrent joy and relief at the sight of them that I remember throughout my childhood and since. As a child I had a recurring nightmare, which seems to be coming true, of the whole world turning into a city. But the knowledge that the woods existed lay behind the images of the cities in which I grew up. My mother had bought a book, at the Presbyterian Missions Book Shop, probably, from which I was to be taught to read. A generously illustrated volume about Indians who lived in the woods and made

canoes. Those people and how they lived so intrigued me that I asked, word by word, what the captions said under the pictures until I could read them myself. I learned to read in order to find out about a woodland people who did not write. I was convinced they were still there.

I did not grow up and go off the live in the actual wilderness. But the love of trees did not leave me, the sense of them as immediate representatives of something immense, desirable, and reassuring. Even the genetically selected, artificially grown individuals set at regular intervals like uniformed humans along the medians of divided highways were a reminder and promise of a life beyond, before, outside human contrivance and assumptions, of the existence of the forest. I needed the knowledge that the forest was there, on the one hand, and I needed human speech on the other. In my case, at least, I believe that the need for both of them is not merely the result of having grown up in cities but is part of the fatal ambiguity of being human.

The notion that the world is divided into city and country (with one of them considered more real than the other) no doubt goes back to the beginning of agriculture and the settling down of groups of humans beside denuded places marked off from the rest of the earth. For some of us, one of the powerful lures of what is called "the country" is the chance to live near trees. And I have never been able to imagine living in the country without having some kind of garden. The practice and art of gardening are remarkably pure forms of the element of paradox underlying all human art and language. A plant in a garden is at once the natural world itself and an object of human arrangement. In a garden we draw something of nonhuman life into our history. When we look at the wilderness we can see it as a place without time, something complete as it is. But looking at a garden, some of its recent evolution, the human intent behind it, is likely to be evident. A past that we recognize. A deliberated present. And of course a gardener is always seeing the garden as a future, something it is supposed to be turning into. Only occasionally can we see the garden itself as something complete, and a moment later we are likely to realize the evanescence of what we are seeing, the brevity of the cherished arrangement.

Carl Linnaeus, Swedish botanist, zoologist and physician

The sense of mortality of each moment of the garden is akin to something that in our time may come to us from any glimpse of wilderness: a stab of anguish, striking from the certainty that we are seeing it for the only time, that somewhere a plan is already in operation—a machine is on its way—to destroy it. I cannot know whether true natives of what we think of as the wilderness are prone to a sense of its fragility or to craving for its presence, but I doubt it. I would be surprised to learn that they considered it particularly beautiful, as someone may whose relation to it includes separation. For I would imagine that such people would feel so much a part of the world around them that they would neither feel

drawn to it nor conceive of being away from it. There is no way of knowing, for by now there may be no true natives left in the sense that I am talking about. And if they exist, the moment they learn of a life "outside" and have exchanged communication with it, they must begin to look at their own world with a new ambivalence, the beginning of a longing and anguish that to us seems old.

I have watched gardens come and go since I was a child, and some of them I thought of as mine. The first one I dug and tended was in a city, in a vacant lot that in times forgotten—a century before—had been woodland. I helped grow peas, lettuce, radishes, corn, tomatoes. For years I loved gardens in Europe, above all the peasant gardens in small villages, and I learned from them most of what I know about growing anything. I used to dream, when I returned to New York, that I had a suitcase full of lettuce seedlings and had to find somewhere to plant them right away.

It was many years before I found my way to the tropics again, the real tropics this time: southern Mexico first, then the windward coast of Hawaii. At the beginning the elation I felt at the sight of the heavy curtains of green and shadow was tempered by a certain reserve, a northern hesitation to acknowledge that what I was seeing was real, in the same way that the tamed woods of Europe or the spindly second and third growth that is all that remains in many parts of the United States are real. I loved what I saw and what it suggested and yet I felt somehow shy and estranged, and it was a while before some center of gravity of mine woke up at home in the tropics, and I understood what had moved the Swedish botanist Linnaeus to say, "Man *dwells* naturally

16

within the tropics and lives on the fruit of the palm tree. He *exists* in other parts of the world and there makes shift to feed on corn and flesh." A statement valuable less for its anthropological accuracy than for its excited intimation of homecoming.

For me as for Linnaeus, if the tropics had meant primarily cities, I would not have stayed. On the other hand, when I walk out of the house it is not into the forest but into a garden. There have been countless notions of what a garden is since the beginning, which some myths represent as a garden. The variations have to do with what the age and its gardeners have thought of as the ideal relation with the wilderness, how they conceived of the role in it of their own artifice—what the great medieval Japanese garden designer Muso called "the making of mountains and rivers." He made some of his waterfalls of stone and some of his pools of moss. They bear something of the same relation to the mountains and rivers outside the gardens that a figure in a painting may bear to its subject. Model to model.

My wish is for a garden that suggests on its own scale the forest, indeed the rain forest. And I recall descriptions I have read of the approaches to Taoist monasteries, where the traveler on the mountain path noticed that the forest seemed to become more beautiful, richer in the dense harmony of things growing there and the enticing perspectives among the trees, and then came to see that the path had become paved with stone and was the way through a garden.

In Hawaiian there is a name for each night of the moon. If I walk out when the moon is up, often I try to remember the name for the night, as though it would

W.S. Merwin 1978

tell me more about what I was seeing. Invariably, I fail, and stand looking at something I can remember no name for.

I come before an extended fan of moonlight four or five feet across, raying out in accordion pleats to pointed tips at the edges. It is one of the leaves of a palm half again as tall as I am now, and when I see it or think of it, names rise to tell me I know it, whatever that means. It is the first Hawaiian palm I planted, or rather the first one that survived. The genus *Pritchardia*, to which all Hawaiian palms belong, contains forty species more or less, depending on which botanist you are consulting. All but four or five of them are native to the Hawaiian chain from the uninhabited island of Niihau far to the north-west, isolated in the Pacific, where a grove of *Pritchardia remota* has evolved on its own in damp earth at the foot of a cliff, to the *P. beccariana* and *P. affinis* of the island of Hawaii, farther to the south. They vary from species such as the *P. gaudichaudii* and *P. martii*, which seldom grow taller than twelve or fifteen feet, to giants like the *P. hardyiana* and *P. schattaueri*, which may reach heights of ninety feet or more, with crowns over twenty feet across. The leaves of all of them are broad elegant fans, and the Hawaiians called them all *loulu*, making no distinction among the species. They used the full grown leaves as umbrellas (for which they are well suited) and as toboggans for sliding down steep slopes into pools below waterfalls, or into the sea.

The botanical names of course belong to the labors of daylight. Often they do no more than identify and are merely eponymous. The name of the genus *Pritchardia* commemorates W. T. Pritchard, a British governor

of Fiji in the last century, and many of the species are named not for their own traits but for the botanists who studied them. In any case the names mean nothing to the trees, and little to most people unless they have reached the point of wanting to tell one kind of palm from another, a degree of interest which sometimes is treated as though it were a little unnatural. The tree in front of me is called a *Pritchardia hillebrandii*, after a German botanist who lived in Honolulu in the 1850s and whose private garden there became the core of the present Honolulu Botanical Garden. The species comes from the island of Moloka'i and there is some doubt as to whether it still exists in the wild state or survives only in cultivation.

Such a doubt is part of why I wanted to plant a tree like this in the first place, though its beauty would have been reason enough, for the *pritchardias* comprise a singularly imposing and elegant group of palms— indeed there are those who insist that they are the most beautiful genus of all. But when young they are virtually impossible to tell apart, and to me, at the beginning, they were simply *loulus*. The wish to plant them was part of a project to grow all the native Hawaiian species I could, to help preserve them. It was an amateur and thoroughly inexpert enterprise but it seemed worth the effort. Hawaiian flora, like the birds of the islands, has suffered appalling losses in the two centuries since European contact. It is said that more animal and plant species have been lost in the islands than in the whole of North America, and many more are endangered. Some native species are not easy to grow and are hopelessly choosy about the conditions they require. But I

Pritchardia Hillebrandii, a native Hawaiian palm

continued to try, and as the *loulus* began to spread their leaves I became addicted to palms.

To other *Pritchardias* first. But the impulse to help save threatened species came rapidly to include flora from other parts of the tropics, especially palms. The Hawaiian ecosystem has been so disturbed and depleted by now, and so many importations have been established (some with very unfortunate results), that although species and enclaves may be preserved, one cannot hope to restore a lost purity of Hawaiian flora in most places. But the danger to living plants throughout the tropics has become common knowledge, and growing even a few individuals in cultivation may be a way of extending the survival of a species. I have been told that Hawaiian species gathered by botanists on Cook's voyages and taken to England to be grown at Kew Gardens subsequently become extinct in Hawaii, and that it was possible to restore them to the islands late from plants growing at Kew. The garden healing the forest.

That can be called justification, and no one who loves music or painting, roses or animals, feels the need to justify it. Such devotions are subjective by nature, and cannot altogether be accounted for. It is impossible to tell someone what you see in a painting or in a garden if they do not see anything there themselves. Coming to see growing things, not as a scientist but as an heir to good fortune, is probably very different from coming to see painting or architecture or any kind of human artifact, and in our age it may be just as independent of considerations of immediate purpose and profit and just as prone to quicken and renew a perennial sense of fullness.

At the same time the growing of anything is a very practical, day-to-day matter, like cooking. The first *Pritchardia hillebrandiis* I grew were gifts from a friend in the local State Department of Land and Natural Resources, Bob Hobdy, who has a detailed knowledge of Hawaiian flora and a deep concern for its survival. Other species of *Pritchardia*, and then of palms from other parts of the world, came as seedlings from botanical gardens and from other gardeners within the islands, and many other seeds from botanical gardens and seed gatherers in Sri Lanka, Java, Taiwan, Japan, Papua New Guinea, the Solomon Islands, Fiji, Australia, Peru, and many other places, and from the Seed Bank of the International Palm Society. With them, and their quarantine documents, has come a correspondence that in some cases is as tantalizing as the seeds: glimpses of people around the globe who are infected with the same palm fever. I keep learning from other gardeners and from my own mistakes the secrets of germinating particular species and bringing them up.

The allure of palms, what to an addict seems to be their peculiar beauty, clearly has something to do with recognition, and so with knowledge. The known age of the family of palms bears a kind of authority, the testament of an ancient order. The record of fossil pollens shows that palms have been palms since the Cretaceous Era, at least sixty million years ago. But that is still a rather intellectual consideration.

Seeing them means, among other things, coming to distinguish them. To begin with, I thought they all looked alike. Now, because they are in a garden and not in the wild, I see (by daylight) other species of

Coconut Palm, *Cocos nucifera*

Pritchardia from other islands, and near them the *Cryosophilas* from the Mexican rainforest with their leaves like green stars, white underneath. Their neighbors here and there, the slender *Chamaedoreas* and the delicately pleated *Geonomas,* a *Neodypsis* from Madagascar, an *Attalea* from South America that may live to rise above everything around it, *Arengas* from Indonesia that tremble in the wind. The variety is enormous. There are between four and five thousand known species, and more are discovered all the time. In no genus, perhaps, is the variation more striking than in the shade-loving *Pinangas* from southeast Asia, growing here downhill from the house under tall mango trees, their leaves mottled in shades of green running from pale chartreuse to inky stains and their stems and crownshafts beginning to suggest the bright oranges, burgundies, ivories, that they will display before the trees first reveal their brilliant seeds. None of these trees has done that yet, for palms grow slowly and most of those here are only a few years old. But a garden is made of hope, which contributes to its pleasure and its fragility. It cannot be proven, nor clutched, nor hurried. And the hope of a palm garden is to be a palm forest.

28

30

34

43

Rain Light

All day the stars watch from long ago
my mother said I am going now
when you are alone you will be all right
whether or not you know you will know
look at the old house in the dawn rain
all the flowers are forms of water
the sun reminds them through a white cloud
touches the patchwork spread on the hill
the washed colors of the afterlife
that lived there long before you were born
see how they wake without a question
even though the whole world is burning

Rain at Night

This is what I have heard

at last the wind in December
lashing the old trees with rain
unseen rain racing along the tiles
under the moon
wind rising and falling
wind with many clouds
trees in the night wind

after an age of leaves and feathers
someone dead
thought of this mountain as money
and cut the trees
that were here in the wind
in the rain at night
it is hard to say it
but they cut the sacred 'ohias then
the sacred koas then
the sandalwood and the halas
holding aloft their green fires
and somebody dead turned cattle loose
among the stumps until killing time

but the trees have risen one more time
and the night wind makes them sound
like the sea that is yet unknown
the black clouds race over the moon
the rain is falling on the last place

The Shape of Water

The garden, or what my wife and I have come to call the garden, follows a small winding valley on the north coast of the Hawaiian island of Maui. Half a mile or so beyond our property line on the seaward side, the stream bed that is the keel of the valley emerges from under a thicket of pandanus trees into a grassy hollow at the top of the sea cliffs, where there was once a watercress pond, and then cuts through the edge to a series of shoulders and shelves and the rocky shoreline.

This is the rainy side of the island and in times of heavy downpours the streambed roars and the muddy torrent can be dangerous, but most of the time there is no water in the channel at all. This part of the coast, whose name in Hawaiian means "fan," is a series of deep sinuous valleys more or less like the one where we live, opening out into basins and then narrowing again into steep gorges filled with dense growth under big trees. Some of these valleys still have their water, or a remnant of it, and the relation of the watercourses to their water is the central thread of the history of the whole area since it was first settled, and most obviously during the past two hundred years. The flow of water in the channel of massive boulders at the bottom of our garden was certainly more constant before the first irrigation ditches and tunnels were carved out of the mountainside above here over a hundred years ago, and before the serpentine coast road was cut through to Hana after the First World War. The rural life of the Hawaiians had always assumed an unfailing supply of pure water, and when the water in these valleys was cut off or severely reduced, the people who lived here, growing taro in flooded terraces surrounded by bananas and sugar cane, people whose forebears had planted the ancestors of the huge mango trees that still shade the stream bed, could no longer survive and were forced to leave.

In the time that I have been acquainted with this region I have become increasingly aware of it as a testament of water, the origin and guide of its contours and gradients and of all the lives—the plants and small creatures and the culture—that evolved here. That was always here to be seen, of course, and the recognition has forced itself, in one form or another, upon people in every part of the world who have been directly involved with the growing of living things. The gardener who ignores it is soon left with no garden. When Alexander Pope, that happily obsessed gardener, urged his reader, in a line that soon became famous, to "Consult the Genius of the Place in all,"

Muso Soseki

the primary office of that Genius as he conceived it was to tell "the Waters or to rise, or fall." The role of water is inseparable from the character of a garden, and even its absence in a garden can take many forms. Muso Soseki, the great thirteenth-century garden designer and poet, directed water with great variety through the gardens he laid out, some of which still survive, but he was also a master of creating the suggestion of non-existent water with bare stones or steep shapes of rock, or foliage or shadows or sand, and long after his death, where

moss has grown over certain of his arrangements, it has continued and deepened the illusion.

When I first saw this valley and these ridges, the water I was most conscious of was the sea itself, the vast expanse of brilliant moving blue stretching north to the horizon beyond which, I knew, there was no land before Alaska. Seen from the house and from the slopes of the garden now, over the leaves of the heliconias and through the fronds of palms, it is the background, both visibly and in time and space, for this island is a mountain—indeed two mountains that rose from the sea and are returning to it. As long as the trades are blowing from the north and east, it is above the sea that the vast ranges of clouds build up, bring to this coast the rain that formed the valleys, made possible the forests all along the mountain, and allowed particular species of plants and insects, tiny brilliant tree snails and birds to evolve for each variation in the terrain. The rain was one of the salient attributes of the early Hawaiian god Lono, the divinity of the growing world who initiates each year of growth when the Pleiades, which in Hawaiian is The Little Eyes, rise above the horizon. In the poetry of the Hawaiians rain almost always is the rain of a particular place, with a specific character and an allusion to an erotic element of some story draped with names. The garden waits for the rain, responds to it at once, opens to it, holds it, takes it up and shines with it. The sound and touch and smell of the rain, the manner of its arrival, its temper and passage are like a sensuous visit to the garden, and the light among the trees after rain, with its own depth and moment, iridescent,

Apple bananas

shifting and unseizable, is an intensified image of the garden at that instant.

But what I saw on the dry afternoon when I first picked my way down the pot-holed track toward the promontory here was the bare ridge thinly covered with long parched grass and scrub guavas thrashing in the trades, and the dust blowing. It was the end of summer

Early sugar cane farming with mules on Maui
(Courtesy Alexander and Baldwin Sugar Museum)

and the rising notes of plovers just back from Alaska for the winter flew in the wind. There were few buildings and they were small and tentative in the glaring light, and there were almost no trees on the upper slopes. I did not know then that the whole coast had been a forest until some time in the last century, its principal trees the great Hawaiian *Acacia koa* and the 'ohia sacred to the fire goddess Pele, the maker of the islands in the first place, and the pandanus and the Hawaiian fan palm, the *loulu*, of the genus Pritchardia, which still grows in small stands in the rain forest to the east along the coast. All of the area was deforested by enterprising Caucasians, first for grazing imported cattle, then for planting sugar, to which the gradients were unsuited. After the road was hacked out above the coast a group of deluded speculators undertook to transform these slopes into a pineapple plantation. They plowed the sides of the valley vertically so that whatever topsoil had remained until then was washed away in a few years and the entrepreneurs lost their investments and left. If I had known what to look for on that first afternoon I would have been able to note the shallow parallel indentations running down through the waving grass across the valley like ripples in sand, the scars of that ruinous venture. I walked down the slope through the scrub and came to the dark green clouds of the mango trees, and under them, in the shade, caught a glimpse of another world.

Even choked, as it was then, with thickets of rampant introduced weed growth, it was the shadowy stream bed with its rocks under the huge trees that made me want to stay and so to settle, and have a garden in this valley. But also the thought of having a chance to take a piece of abused land and restore it to some capacity of which I had only a vague idea was part of the appeal, and the day I signed the escrow papers for the land I planted, up along the ridge, the first trees of a windbreak.

From the beginning I wanted to use native species and try to bring back some of the growth that would have covered these slopes if they had been left undisturbed. I knew it would be an arduous undertaking but it was also far more complex than I could have imagined. I did manage to find and establish a number of indigenous kinds of trees and plants, and I think that when I began I still supposed that humans could "reforest" when in fact all we can do is to plant this or that and hope that what we are doing turns out to be appropriate. Plainly I had been making my way toward such an intimation, and toward the present garden, since I was a small child in Union City, New Jersey, drawn by an inexplicable cluster of feelings as by a magnet, to tufts of grass appearing between cracks in the stone slabs of the sidewalk. When I was nine we moved to Scranton, Pennsylvania. I thought then that I knew what a garden was. There was the one my mother made under the kitchen window along a few feet of brick walk with portulaca, irises, larkspur, cosmos, and a red rambler on the green picket fence by the alley. And there was the Victory Garden that we made in the coal company's empty lot across the alley, after a man came at the end of winter and managed to get a horse and an old plow up over the stone curb and through the gate in the cast-iron fence and plowed up the space while I watched him, as though he were someone I had read about. In Europe and in Mexico, wherever I had lived I had tended gardens with no particular skill, and had loved them, and been fed by them, but most of my questions to do with them had been practical ones, for most of them were in places that had been thought of as

Merwin as a child with palm

gardens by other people for a long time. It was here on a tropical island, on ground impoverished by human use and ravaged by a destructive history, that I found a garden that raised questions of a different kind—including what a garden really was after all, and what I thought I was doing in it.

Obviously a garden is not the wilderness but an assembly of shapes, most of them living, that owes some share of its composition, its appearance, to human design and effort, human conventions and convenience, and the human pursuit of that elusive, indefinable harmony that we call beauty. It has a life of its own, an intricate, willful, secret life, as any gardener knows. It is only the humans in it who think of it as a garden. But a garden is a relation, which is one of the countless reasons why it is never finished.

I have admired and have loved gardens of many kinds, but what I aspire to, and want to have around our lives now, is a sense of the forest. It must be an illusion of the forest, clearly, for this is a garden and so a kind of fiction. But the places in the garden where I find myself lingering and staring with unsoundable pleasure are those where it looks to me as though—with the shafts of light reaching and dividing through the trees—it might be deep in the forest. Years ago I read of gardens around Taoist monasteries in the mountains of China, gardens that seemed to be the forest itself into which the mountain paths wound and the traveler discovered that the forest at every turn looked more beautiful, the perspectives and forms and the variety of greens and shadows and flowers more wonderful, and then it became

apparent that the mossed stones of the path had been arranged there, and a turn brought glimpses of a low wall and bit of monastery roof appearing like a shoulder of the hillside. Behind my own fiction, I suppose, is the fond belief that something of the kind can exist.

When we have reached a point where our own kind is steadily destroying the rest of the life on earth and some of us are anxious not to do that, our relation to the earth begins to be that of a gardener to a garden. I believe that gardening, the deliberate influencing of particular plants in the forest, existed for millennia before there was agriculture, and I am convinced that there was a measure of joy and magic in that relation from the beginning, something that probably sobered up considerably when it started to fall into line and become agriculture.

Such considerations turn up around me as I try to find out what the garden—this garden—may be. They raise further questions, such as the prospects for indigenous and endemic species in circumstances that have been radically altered, the particular advisability or risks of calculated or accidental introductions—plants, insects, birds, animals, including ourselves. I want a garden that is an evolving habitat in which a balance is constantly being sought and found between responsibility and provisional control.

But I certainly do not want to suggest that the garden is an earnest duty, a program of moral calisthenics undertaken like an hour at an exercise machine. If I hear the word *yardwork* I avoid the subject. For the person who has arrived at gardening at whatever age, it is an enchantment, all of it, from the daydreaming to the digging, the heaving, the weeding and watching and watering, the heat, and the stirrings at the edges of the days.

Some gardens of course are communal activities, but much gardening is quiet work and a good deal of it is done alone. I have been describing my own ruminations about the garden, but my wife Paula and I work in it together. Part of the time on the same thing, much of the time on our own. Either way, it is what we are both doing.

Some of the things growing here now were already in the ground before we met, but it was only after it was clear that Paula wanted to live here too, after thirty years in New York, that what is around us began to be not simply an assembly of plants laboriously set into soil and conditions that had been rendered inhospitable for many of them, but a garden. Her lack of hesitation was less surprising to her than it was to me. She was born in Argentina, grew up in the tropics, and had always wanted a garden, read about gardens, imagined living in a garden. She had not been here for more than a day or two before she was out on the slope dragging long grass from around young plantings and helping to clear space for others.

Different parts of the garden have different forms. There is the food garden, a number of raised beds and a curving screen of banana trees, that supplies something or other—lemons, limes, papayas, salad, peppers, eggplant, sweet potatoes, maybe corn—for the meals of most days. But I am afraid that gets less than its share

of attention regularly as a result of the allurements of growing other things. Above all palms. The inaugural ambition to proliferate native species has endowed us with several kinds of native hibiscus, Hawaiian artemisia, trees ranging from seedlings to tall figures on the upland areas, but it came to focus on Hawaiian palms, some highly endangered (one, on the island of Molokai, is reduced to a single tree in the wild). Most of the species now exist in the garden, and growing them from seeds led to a fascination with palms from elsewhere, and with cycads and other flora of the world's increasingly menaced tropics, and an attempt to make a situation where they might be able to live as though they belonged together, here in this part of this valley.

Limes

A visitor to a garden sees the successes, usually. The gardener remembers mistakes and losses, some for a long time, and imagines the garden in a year, and in an unimaginable future. There are young trees in the ground. The days are much too short, they go by too fast, and we wish for rain and the sound of water among the rocks.

59

66

Native Trees

Neither my father nor my mother knew
the names of the trees
where I was born
what is that
I asked and my
father and mother did not
hear they did not look where I pointed
surfaces of furniture held
the attention of their fingers
and across the room they could watch
walls they had forgotten
where there were no questions
no voices and no shade

Were there trees
where they were children
where I had not been
I asked
were there trees in those places
where my father and my mother were born
and in that time did
my father and my mother see them
and when they said yes it meant
they did not remember
What were they I asked what were they
but both my father and my mother
said they never knew

To Lili's Walk

Strange that now there should be no sign of you
visible on the dusty way between
the shadows where the morning light comes through
to lie across those places we have been
time and again though at the other end
of the day when the sun was nearly gone
and from the other side the beams lengthened
under the trees where you kept setting one
foot down carefully before the other
weaving upstream along with me to where
we would go no farther then together
and I said you know the way back from there
I will wait and you can follow alone
and between us the night has come and gone

The House and Garden

The Emergence of a Dream

The small valley of Peahi Stream is on the north coast of the island of Maui. It is often referred to as the "windward" coast in the weather forecasts: it is the rainy coast, with sea cliffs rather than beaches. The weather pattern and the paucity of beaches spared it from development until recent years. The north coast cliffs face out into the trade winds, which we love, and which bring—however unevenly—the blessed rain. I had come to Maui, after some months in Honolulu, in order to study with Robert Aitken, a Zen teacher whom I had met on O'ahu. For several months I lived in a couple of rooms above an outbuilding, up among the banana trees beside Robert and Anne Aitken's house, until I found somewhere of my own to rent a few miles away. There were not as many houses in "upcountry" Maui then as there are now. The road that led past the Aitkens' house had been unpaved until earlier that year. It was very quiet and seemed to be part of an earlier time, and I loved that, imagining that it would stay that way.

The house I found to rent had been knocked together by one of the many "rough carpenters" who were trying to improvise a livelihood around Maui in those days. They had come to Maui, many of them in their twenties, as surfers. The house they had built was as makeshift as their lives. Their former residence, a truck-camper shell, sat out in the long grass between the house and the neighboring pasture. The house was built out of odds and ends of material salvaged from buildings that were being demolished somewhere else. The roof was made of corrugated metal and must have been the first one the builders had ever laid, because they had set all the nails in the valleys of the already-rusted metal sheets so that when it rained, water flowed in through all the nail holes. The winter rains began just as I moved in, and it was a very rainy winter. Before long I was living out of plastic bags kept up on chairs. The house had a glorious view of the whole isthmus of central Maui, with the sea on both sides and the west Maui mountain, Pu'u Eke, with its peak hidden in clouds, beyond them. I made friends along the road, but I kept looking for somewhere else.

Then a friend told me of a bit of land out on the coast with a small cabin on it. I was told it was out in the wilds, like a bit of frontier country. My friend said the cabin was where three of the native Hawaiian activists had hidden after they left the bombed island of Kaho'olawe, which they had occupied in defiance of the U.S. Navy, which had been using the island for bombing practice. The present owner wanted to sell the place, and I went to look.

It was down a rough dirt road that looked like one of the cane truck roads through the sugar and pineapple fields. It wound its way toward the ocean. A mile below the main road, which had only recently been paved that far out from town, as I was threading my way across potholes and over rocks, I heard plovers sailing overhead in pairs. I was hearing the same clear, rising notes that they called to each other on their long migration flights at night over the sea. That sound was the first thing about the place that caught me, like the note of a bell. I passed only two buildings, set back from the dirt track, on the way down. One of them looked like an old caboose with a tiny upper room perched on top of

it, and there was another a short distance beyond that, half-hidden over a ridge.

The directions I was following led me to a pair of tree trunk fence posts set back from the road like gate posts, on the left, and no gate. No fence either. There were no fences along that road. I drove in between the two posts to where the ruts stopped a few steps from the cabin. There were no trees except for a few scraggly guavas, hardly more than bushes. Beyond the cabin was a long slope covered with dry grass. Along its lower edge were some small trees that I would come to know as Christmasberries—an imported weed tree—and below them the tops of larger trees. The wind blowing across the ridge behind me framed the silence. I learned later that, in state assessments of agricultural land, the land there had been pronounced wasteland, ruined beyond agricultural use, after little more than a century of abusive exploitation. Until the early nineteenth century there had been a forest there, its dominant tree the Hawaiian koas (*Acacia koa*) accompanied by 'ohias (*Metrosideros polymorpha*) and other native trees and shrubs, including, perhaps, native palms of the genus Pritchardia. On this coast there would have been the very beautiful Pritchardia arecina, which grow now in small numbers in the high forests of the eastern end of the island. The land here had been deforested as early as the 1840s, some trees cut for firewood for the whaling ships that put in at the harbor of Lahaina on the south side of the island, and for the new population of American and European settlers there.

The deforestation had been hastened in order to provide pasture for cattle, but the wild grasses that grew up here provided poor grazing. When sugarcane planting began in midcentury, the first big planters, in heated competition with each other, planted cane fields wherever they thought sugar would grow, and competed furiously for all available water along the north coast. In the course of their diversion of every stream and runoff along the coast to irrigate their cane fields in the central plain, the water of the stream here—Peahi Stream— had been cut off completely.

The planters had plowed the land for sugar wherever they could, far beyond the central isthmus. But the yield out along the coast proved not to pay for the growing, and the fields were abandoned. The plowing had accelerated the erosion begun by the cutting of the trees. Then the land reverted to poor pasture for some years, and in the early twentieth century a group of hopeful speculators who had watched the introduction of large-scale pineapple growing decided to go in for it themselves, and they pooled their resources and bought most of the valley, intending to grow pineapple on the slopes. For some reason hard to imagine, they plowed the slopes vertically—up and down—which of course greatly accelerated the erosion. In the winter rains the land lost what little topsoil had survived the earlier abuses, the speculators gave up the whole business, and the land stood idle for decades. Wasteland. The building of the road to Hana in the 1920s further sealed off the upper sources of the Peahi Stream. In the 1970s the slopes were divided on a map and sections put up for sale. They were still classified as "agricultural land."

The section on which the cabin stood consisted of slightly over three acres. It was not hard to see that the soil was poor. If I had known to look for them I would have been able to see the up-and-down corduroy ridges in the dry, waving grass across the valley, a testament of the most recent land abuse. But the condition of the soil did not, in itself, daunt me. I had long dreamed of having a chance one day to try to restore a bit of the earth's surface that had been abused by human "improvement." I loved the wind-swept ridge, empty of the sounds of

A mule drawn plow in sugar cane field, Maui, c. 1920
(Courtesy Maui Historical Society)

machines, just as it was, with its tawny, dry grass waving in the wind of late summer. The rough road behind me and the one along the top of the ridge on the other side of the valley led down to end at the sea cliff a quarter of a mile away. I had not yet seen that the road on which I had come ended on a headland, overlooking a large bay

with a shore of boulders and a hill behind that on which the second-largest heiau (Hawaiian temple platform and compound) in the islands, wholly unexcavated, was hidden under mango trees.

I was captivated by the sense of distance along the coast. From in front of the cabin there was only one other building to be seen: a barn-red house halfway down the opposite slope. Out beyond the sea cliffs the ocean extended without a break all the way to Alaska. That was the destination, every spring, of the migrating plovers that flashed above me far ahead of their call-notes. From the cabin on that first day I followed the ghost of a path down through the waist-high grass. It curved to the left and then swung to lead down under the mango trees. When I stepped into their shade I seemed at once to be in another world. The sound of the wind was suddenly muted and far away. The air was cooler, and from somewhere I could not see among the trees I was startled to hear the voice of a thrush singing at that hour of the day. It was the omao, known as the "Hawaiian thrush," though in fact it was a foreigner, just as I was. It was also called, more accurately, the Chinese thrush, and also the Laughing thrush. There are few members of the thrush family, whatever their species, that are not great singers (the American robin is a notable exception) and the omao, like the nightingale, never repeats itself but sings variations from an inexhaustible source. I stood still and listened, looking along the valley in the shade of the mango trees as the thrush went on singing, and then I stepped down the slope and walked over to the rocky stream bed itself. I stood there hearing the thrush and wanting to stay there.

No story begins at the beginning. The beginning does not belong to knowledge. I have been asked fairly often how I came to care about living things that are not human—for all that is commonly referred to as "nature." There is a suggestion sometimes that a sympathy of that kind is somehow eccentric. Such use of the word "nature" seems to refer to something apart from "us." Yet the sympathy seems to me natural, even if the overt first impulse of living organisms is rarely generous. I cannot remember a time when I did not feel that attraction, that delight in lives that were not human. I have a vivid recollection of one moment of it when I must have been hardly more than two years old. I was walking with my mother along the sidewalk on New York Avenue outside our house in Union City, New Jersey. Sidewalks then were commonly made of flagstones. Right outside our own picket fence I saw, between two flagstones, tender new shoots of grass so young that the light passed through them. It must have been spring. I bent down to look and I asked my mother where the grass was coming from. I remember my happiness, the sense of reassurance I felt when she told me that the earth was right under there.

When I first saw farmland and woods as a child, I wanted to be there, to get out of the car or the train and be surrounded by what I saw. My mother read the words from picture books to my younger sister and me before we could read, and there was one book in particular that I kept returning to on my own because of its subject. It was a book about Indians living in the woods, and there were watercolors of the woodlands and of their life there that drew me back with a kind

One of the early palms planted

of longing. There were few words on the first pages. I looked at them again and again, and with my mother's help I managed to learn to recognize the letters for "man," then "an Indian man," and then where he was and what he was doing, and it was as though it were coming to life in front of me. I was learning to read in order to know about people who did not read or write but who lived all the time in the woods. I said that was what I wanted to do. The wish of a child, but it stayed with me all through my childhood.

I mentioned earlier that I had come to Maui, in the first place, principally in order to spend some time learning about Zen practice under the guidance of Robert Aitken, whose Maui Zendo was on a back road along the north coast of the island. That, and a growing fondness for Maui, had kept me here. My attraction to the image of the Chinese mountain temples and monasteries in John Blofeld's account, and how they appeared to have grown out of their surroundings without intruding upon them, came from the same part of my own temperament. It seemed that I had been searching for something of the kind all my life. That desire influenced the site I chose for the house, and then its design and floor plan.

Although I began with a naïve aspiration to restore a few acres of pure Hawaiian rainforest, the first trees I planted here were not indigenous to Hawaii. No native trees would grow in the parched, windswept conditions and the leached-out soil, as they were then, up along the ridge. I planted Cassuarinas, known locally as "ironwoods," beautiful trees that look like tall, weeping pines and were named by the seventeenth-century botanist

Rumphius for the Cassowary bird with its long, graceful wings. But the whole genus has acquired a bad name in Hawaii because the first species planted here was aggressively invasive, sending up outriders from its running surface roots. I was careful to plant species that had no such intrusive habits and were especially graceful. Even in the conditions here they grew rapidly, and within a few years they began to form a miniclimate as they shaded the ground, added humus with their fallen needles, held the water after heavy rains, and put nitrogen back into the soil—they are one of very few genera besides the legumes that can do that. They broke the wind with a lovely sound, their long limbs swaying. No one seemed to know at the beginning that they were vulnerable to termites, and eventually they began to be infested and to drop large limbs. Now they are being replaced, in the habitat they improved, by young palms.

The conditions of the land here discouraged the possibility of restoring Hawaiian native flora. There was a forest here in the early nineteenth century with its dominant tree, the beautiful *Acacia koa*, and we planted many seedling koas, but very few of them survived. The disturbance of the soil apparently had been too great. It had been leached out and was unwelcoming to what had once grown there. It must have lost a whole society of soil organisms and forms of life in which the native trees and plants had once grown, and now instead there were insects and plant ailments that had not existed until that land was deforested. Of the few koas we planted that survived and prospered, almost every one was killed suddenly by imported weevils or diseases. Some other native species have not done well here either, but the

first indigenous palms I planted here in soil carefully amended with rotted manure and seaweed, which settled in and grew and allowed some hope, were Hawaiian palms. As they grew and I began to learn about them, I came to realize that palms, which grow in extremely diverse conditions all around the world, are endangered, like so many other living things everywhere, by human takeover of their habitats, and I wanted to try to see what palms would grow here in circumstances that, on the one hand, were not totally artificial, and on the other, might resemble, insofar as possible, those from which they had come. I had planted the first palms here very soon after I had signed the deed for the land in 1977.

The ones I cared about most were the Hawaiian *Pritchardias*, acquired from a friend a couple of miles away who had a small nursery of indigenous plants. They were a few years old, in three-gallon pots, when I bought them from him. I began corresponding with palm growers and botanical gardeners in other parts of the tropics and learned from reading how to grow palms from seed, which I did with a success that varied with the freshness of the seeds, among other things.

It was an exciting time, and the palms I managed to grow, and the emerging garden, added to our attachment to our life here. Then three years after Paula had first come here, the two parcels of land adjoining ours on the side away from the sea suddenly became available to us. They belonged to two elderly women over on O'ahu, one of whom—with the parcel nearer to us—we had already approached and had visited several times. She had encouraged us, but said she would not sell the land as long as her husband was alive. After he died,

she and the woman who owned the plot next to hers were ready to sell. Their combined two plots amounted to over fifteen acres and contained the whole of the upper bed of Peahi Stream. The women knew that we did not want the land for development but to preserve it from that and to try to make a kind of botanical sanctuary there. They were less interested in acquiring the highest possible price than in immediate cash, and they agreed to sell to us for a figure that was remarkably low even at that time. An old friend of mine only a few months earlier had left me a sum of money, to my surprise, and a friend of Paula's, an older woman who had been a kind of godmother of hers for many years, gave her a sum, too, and we combined them to pay cash for those two parcels of land. It was a piece of fortune that came to us like a blessing.

With no irrigation system, I have relied upon planting palms as far as possible in rainy periods, digging holes as large as possible and filling them with mixes of compost and organic fertilizers and watering them by hand for a while when the rains stop. It is not an ideal way of doing it, and in periods of drought I lose some recent plantings. I tend to plant palms younger than I believe is usual in professional botanical gardens, where they have watering systems and a staff of gardeners. Keeping palms in the nursery until they are larger and older increases a risk of ailments and ant damage and requires much larger holes, more water after planting, and tends to be a greater shock to the tree than it is when they are set in the ground sooner. In between twenty-five or thirty years I have planted about 850 species of palms, and at least four or five times that many actual trees. I have had no map. I have not been able to visit every planting regularly, nor to water them all by hand. Some have been lost to drought. Labels have been lost. But I would guess that well over seven hundred species and more than three quarters of all the palms that I have set in the ground have survived. They grow slowly in this poor soil, but some of the older ones, planted in the early eighties, are tall and stately now, and many of them are flowering and dropping viable seed. Many endangered species are growing here, and one species in particular, the *Hyophorbe indica* from Reunion Island, was listed as extinct when Inge Hoffinan sent me a few seeds in the 1980s. One remaining tree of the species had been found in the botanical garden on that island, and it had provided those seeds. I managed to grow several trees and eventually began sending the seeds to a palm nursery on the Big Island for distribution, and they are available to tropical gardeners now. During rainy spells I try to plant at least one palm every day. Many have grown out of recognition. I welcomed Chipper Wichman's statement at Kahanu Garden here on Maui that once the Conservancy is in existence he wants the National Tropical Botanical Garden, of which he is the present director, to redocument and map the palms here, and there have been other welcome offers to help record the palms.

I hope to be able to go on planting palms on this land for a long time, and I regard what has been done here so far as just a beginning. The upland areas beyond the streambed and on the western side of the valley have scarcely been planted at all, and I hope—we both hope—that the whole of this land can eventually become a palm garden, a palm forest and sanctuary. Just being here with the garden, the "palm forest," all around us, day after day, I think has taught me a great deal. In my own lifetime I have seen the role of a garden, the very idea of a garden, not merely altered but reversed. Gardens, from the beginning (as the etymology of the word suggests), existed as enclaves designed and maintained to keep out the wilderness, to guard what was inside for human use or pleasure. Once it became possible for human beings to destroy environments anywhere on earth, the situation was turned around, and anyone who wanted to protect and save any remaining bit of the natural environment was acting in the role of a gardener—one whose purpose, at this point, was to keep encroaching human exploitation and disturbance out. The model for this garden has always been the forest itself, even though I know that the word "reforestation" is generally meaningless, and that only a forest knows how to grow a forest.

I hope that the planting of palms will continue to fill parts of the land that have not been planted up until now. I hope that a future head gardener will have something of the same desire that I have had: to try to grow as many species as possible of the world's palms, wherever they can be acquired. That is an abiding part of our hope that a Conservancy will want and will be able to save this bit of the Peahi streambed—what we have made here for those who come after us.

91

99

108

The Laughing Thrush

O nameless joy of the morning

tumbling upward note by note out of the night
and the hush of the dark valley
and out of whatever has not been there

song unquestioning and unbounded
yes this is the place and the one time
in the whole of before and after
with all of memory waking into it

and the lost visages that hover
around the edge of sleep
constant and clear
and the words that lately have fallen silent
to surface among the phrases of some future
if there is a future

here is where they all sing the first daylight
whether or not there is anyone listening

To Paula in Late Spring

Let me imagine that we will come again
when we want to and it will be spring
we will be no older than we ever were
the worn griefs will have eased like the early cloud
through which the morning slowly comes to itself
and the ancient defenses against the dead
will be done with and left to the dead at last
the light will be as it is now in the garden
that we have made here these years together
of our long evenings and astonishment

Place

On the last day of the world
I would want to plant a tree

what for
not for the fruit

the tree that bears the fruit
is not the one that was planted

I want the tree that stands
in the earth for the first time

with the sun already
going down

and the water
touching its roots

in the earth full of the dead
and the clouds passing

one by one
over its leaves

I first met William Merwin in 1992 while working on a film project for the University of South Carolina. Dr. John Carpenter from USC's Center for Science Education was interested in producing a film series about the convergence of the sciences and the humanities. The hope was to expand the audience for environmental education by merging science research with writing, music, and the arts. The idea of a writer, especially a poet, was a good fit and Merwin was a natural choice. While there were many wonderful writers to consider— Peter Mattiessen, Barry Lopez, Terry Tempest Williams and others—I had a connection to Merwin's writing that I cannot explain adequately to this day.

Like many others, I first encountered Merwin's poetry in an undergraduate American Literature class. The first poem I recall reading was "For a Coming Extinction," a poem I still keep close to me (I have a broadside of the poem on the wall of our home). I remember sitting on the lanai of his home that first afternoon, overlooking the garden and onward to the sea, and attempting to explain to him why I wanted to produce a film about his work. I recall saying something about his poems giving voice to things I had felt all my life but never had the words for. The "sound of paws in high grass," "a kind of whispered sighing not far like a night wind in pines," "eyes fashioned of the most precious of metals." When I read his poems, it is always part discovery and part recollection, like some long buried memory rising to the surface.

Thankfully, William agreed to the project and the film "Witness" was completed in 1995. Since that time, we have maintained contact through letters, short visits at poetry readings during his annual reading tours, and through the infrequent trips to Maui. Over the years, I watched the garden grow to include over three thousand palms and over eight hundred species, transforming itself into the wildness that William so loves.

This is not the formal courtyard gardens of the South Carolina lowcountry. This is an organic explosion of native and non-native palms, ginger, pandanus, ferns, heliconia, and countless other plants growing in and around each other. While William would rightfully distinguish it from a forest, it has many of the characteristics of one. The plantings are close together and the denseness of the vegetation is magnified by the daily rain, causing the shining branches to drape over each other and ever closer to the ground. Interrupted only by the occasional path for access and maintenance, the garden is a constant surprise. Bromeliads push through the propped roots of halas. Air plants and Spanish moss hang above a floor of ferns and hibiscus. Seeds of every color and shape adorn the paths and branches. Every step along any path surrounds you with a kind of chaos of beauty and color.

Visiting the garden with William and Paula is a walk unlike most garden tours. They seem to remember each plant, its common and Latin name, its country of origin, and how well it gets along with its neighbors. Any walk with them is part pleasure, part maintenance, with dropped branches being picked up along the way and some gentle pruning where necessary. Paula's touch is seen, especially along the paths. Potted succulents and flowers grace the rock-covered steps down the slope and a brass toad marks the turn

to the house. Their love for the garden they have created together is remarkable, much like the love between the two of them. This is not a garden created by a landscape designer—it is a garden created by decades of care with their own hands.

The idea for this book surfaced in the Spring of 2012 when William visited USC to be awarded the Thomas Cooper Medal for Distinction in the Arts and Sciences. The following week, William, Paula, my wife Susan and I had spent the day visiting the small private gardens of Charleston. They were delighted by the gardens and the beauty of the city. Later while walking through White Point Garden, Paula and I began to discuss the possibility of a book of garden photographs and the idea grew from there. The hope was to assemble a collection of essays and poems, accompanied by photographs of the garden that would give the viewer a sense of place. While no collection of photographs can capture the true beauty and complexity of the garden, I hope these images will give the viewer a glimpse into this extraordinary place.

While I enjoyed the support and help of many people during this project, I am especially grateful to my wife, Susan Alexander. Susan shares my love for the garden and for William and Paula. Most of the images in this book were captured with Susan standing beside me, holding a reflector in one hand and an umbrella in the other, always encouraging, always supportive. She took many weeks away from her own work and career to help me with this project. This book is as much her work as it is mine.

The late John H. "Jack" McGrail taught me photography while I was as student at the University of South Carolina back in the 1970s. We remained close until his passing a few years ago. Whenever I thanked Jack for everything that he had done for me, he would channel his gruff, inner Irishman and tell me, "I didn't teach you anything." My answer to him was always the same—"You taught me all I needed to know." Thanks again, Jack.

And, of course, Paula. Paula was the original inspiration for this collaboration. Without her this book would not have happened. During rainy afternoons I would sometimes retreat to the shelter of the lanai. The dogs would announce my arrival, and Paula would emerge from the house. She would always take a break from her own work to sit and talk while the rain fell on the garden. We would talk about small things—the recent sighting of a Brazilian cardinal in the neighborhood or the gecko hiding on the wet ginger just beyond the eaves. When the rain eased, she would slip back into the house while I headed up the path to resume my work, knowing, that with any luck, there would be more rain tomorrow.

In 2010, William and Paula established the Merwin Conservancy (Merwinconservancy.org) to care for the garden once their time as caretakers has passed. The Conservancy's mission is to "preserve the legacy and palm forest of W. S. Merwin and bring his values, as expressed through his work and forest, out into the community through research, education and outreach." It is my hope that this book can help spread the word of this important effort.

To this day I still do not completely understand why William said yes to the film project so many years ago. It certainly wasn't because I was a well-known filmmaker or that I had unlimited resources to support such an effort. But having come to know William over these past twenty years, I have a good idea why he agreed—he did it for me. I think he understood how important it was for me to make the film. He understood this even more than I did.

After the film project was complete, William gave me a signed broadside as a gift. It was of the poem "One Story." The poem closes with:

> but what came out of the forest
> was all part of the story
> whatever died on the way
> or was named but no longer
> recognizable even
> what vanished out of the story
> finally day after day
> was becoming the story
> so that when there is no more
> story that will be our
> story when there is no
> forest that will be our forest

His inscription on the broadside reads: "For your part of the story." In some small way, I hope these photographs are part of my story, part of William's story, part of the garden's story. Whatever beauty is in these photographs is William's beauty, whatever wildness is William's wildness. For helping me with my "part of the story," I am forever in his debt.

KEY TO THE PALMS

62–63   Archontophoenix cunninghamia

75   Archontophoenix purpurea

92   Arenga undulatifolia

77   Astrocaryum alatum

24   Bismarkia nobilis

5   Bismarkia nobilis

10   Cocos nucifera

105   Dypsis lastelliana

4   Dypsis Madagascariensis and Roystonea oleracea

3   Dypsis pembana, grove

106   Dypsis pembana; young trunk

68   Johannesteijsmannia altifrons

40   Licuala paludosa, fruit

25   Licuala paludosa, Pritchardia sp. (above)

6   Licualis grandis and Archontophoenix purpurea

ii–iii   Livistona sp.

67   Phoenicophorium borsigianum

39   Pinanga gracilis

7   Rhapidophyllum hystrix, Arenga undulatifolia

27   Roystonea regia

76   Sabal sp.